I can't see you, God,

   so please give me a clue:

Do you look like me,

   and do I look like you?

Are you big or little?

Are you short or tall?

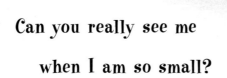

Can you really see me

when I am so small?

Do you like to whisper?

Do you like to shout?

Can you sing or whistle?

I'd like to find out.

Are you strong or gentle?

Are you ever sad?

Do you have a temper
like me when I'm mad?

Where do you live?

In a house in the sky?

How do I know

you are somewhere nearby?

Do you love me always,

or just when I'm good?

I don't always do things

the way that I should.

I have lots of questions

to ask you like these.

I wonder if maybe

you'll answer them, please?

You're looking for answers?

Then here's what to do:

Just turn to the Bible

to find what is true,

And listen to everything

I say to you.

You won't find a picture
of me in a book.

There isn't one person

who knows how I look.

But don't be upset

   that you can't see my face.

You can look at my work

   in this beautiful place!

I've been alive

since before time began;

I made the whole world

by my very own plan.

27

I'm as tall as the heavens;

I'm as wide as the sea.

28

But even your hairs

are all counted by me.

My voice can be gentle

and silent and still,

And also like thunder

that roars through the hills.

I sing with the waves

and the whistling breeze,

And joining my song

are the hills and the trees.

I'm strong as a fortress,

a rock, and a shield,

But as gentle as rain

falling softly on fields.

When you are unhappy

that makes me feel sad.

I'm filled with great joy

when I make your heart glad.

47

My anger comes slowly

and fades like the night.

There's no darkness in me,

just goodness and light.

I live in the world

and in heaven above.

I live in the hearts

of my people who love.

For I AM the maker
of heaven and earth.
I spoke, and my Word
brought all life into birth.

I AM like a mother

who comforts your fears

And tenderly wipes away

all of your tears.

I AM like a father

    who wants to provide,

To care for your needs

    and to stay by your side.

I AM the Creator,

the first and the last,

I'm God of the present,

the future, the past.

I AM the good shepherd,

who cares for each lamb.

I AM the Almighty,

I AM WHO I AM.

I'll love you forever,

whatever you do,

For nothing can separate

my love from you.

I've loved everything

that I made from the start.

My world and my people

I hold in my heart.

Bible References

Here are some Bible verses to talk about as you read this book again with your child. You may want to open your Bible as you read the verses. This will help your little one understand that God's answers in this poem come from his Word, the Bible.

You won't find a picture of me in a book.
There isn't one person who knows how I look.

No one has ever seen God. I JOHN 4:12, NLT

But don't be upset that you can't see my face.
You can look at my work in this beautiful place!

Then God looked over all he had made, and he saw that it was excellent in every way. GENESIS 1:31, NLT

I've been alive since before time began;
I made the whole world by my very own plan.

In the beginning God created the heavens and the earth. GENESIS 1:1, NLT

I'm as tall as the heavens; I'm as wide as the sea.

The sky is no limit for God. . . . God's greatness is broader than the earth, wider than the sea. JOB 11:8-9, TEV

But even your hairs are all counted by me.

And the very hairs on your head are all numbered.
MATTHEW 10:30, NLT

My voice can be gentle and silent and still,

And after the fire there was the sound of a gentle
whisper. I KINGS 19:12, NLT

And also like thunder that roars through the hills.

Listen carefully to the thunder of God's voice as it rolls
from his mouth. JOB 37:2, NLT

I sing with the waves and the whistling breeze,
And joining my song are the hills and the trees.

The voice of the Lord is heard on the seas;
    the glorious God thunders,
    and his voice echoes over the ocean.
The Lord's voice shakes the oaks
    and strips the leaves from the trees.
    PSALM 29:3, 9, TEV

Let the rivers clap their hands in glee!
Let the hills sing out their songs of joy.
    PSALM 98:8, NLT

You live in joy and peace. The mountains and hills will burst into song, and the trees of the field will clap their hands!
ISAIAH 55:12, NLT

I'm as strong as a fortress, a rock, and a shield,

The Lord is my protector;
he is my strong fortress . . .
He protects me like a shield;
he defends me and keeps me safe.
PSALM 18:2, TEV

You have turned from the God who can save you—the Rock who can hide you. ISAIAH 17:10, NLT

But as gentle as rain falling softly on fields.

He will respond to us as surely as the arrival of dawn or the coming of rains in early spring. HOSEA 6:3, NLT

When you are unhappy, that makes me feel sad.

The Lord is near to those who are discouraged;
he saves those who have lost all hope.
PSALM 34:18, TEV

I'm filled with great joy when I make your heart glad.

Find out for yourself how good the Lord is.
Happy are those who find safety with him.
PSALM 34:8, TEV

You have put gladness in my heart. PSALM 4:7, NRSV

My anger comes slowly and fades like the night.

The Lord is slow to anger and rich in unfailing love.
NUMBERS 14:18, NLT

There's no darkness in me, just goodness and light.

God is light and there is no darkness in him at all.
1 JOHN 1:5, NLT

I live in the world and in heaven above.

There is no one like the Lord our God.
He lives in the heights above,
    but he bends down
    to see the heavens and the earth.
PSALM 113:5-6, TEV

I live in the hearts of my people who love.

God is love, and all who live in love live in God, and God lives in them. 1 JOHN 4:16, NLT

For I AM the maker of heaven and earth.
I spoke, and my Word brought all life into birth.

The Lord merely spoke,
and the heavens were created.
He breathed the word,
and all the stars were born.
For when he spoke, the world began!
It appeared at his command.
PSALM 33:6, 9, NLT

I AM like a mother who comforts your fears

You will be like a child that is nursed by its mother, carried in her arms, and treated with love. I will comfort you . . . as a mother comforts her child. ISAIAH 66:12-13, TEV

And tenderly wipes away all of your tears.

And God will wipe away all their tears. REVELATION 7:17, NLT

I AM like a father who wants to provide,

Your heavenly Father already knows all your needs, and he
will give you all you need from day to day.
MATTHEW 6:32–33, NLT

To care for your needs and stay by your side.

I will not be afraid,
for you are close beside me.
Psalm 23:4, NLT

I AM the Creator, the first and the last.
I'm God of the present, the future, the past.

"I am the . . . beginning and the end," says the Lord God.
"I am the one who is, who always was, and who is still to
come, the Almighty One." REVELATION 1:8, NLT

I AM the good shepherd, who cares for each lamb.

The Lord is my shepherd;
I have everything I need.
PSALM 23:1, NLT

He will feed his flock like a shepherd. He
will carry the lambs in his arms, holding
them close to his heart. ISAIAH 40:11, NLT

I AM the Almighty, I AM WHO I AM.

God said, "I am who I am." EXODUS 3:14, TEV

**I'll love you forever, whatever you do,
For nothing can separate my love from you.
I've loved everything that I made from the start.
My world and my people I hold in my heart.**

Can anything ever separate us from Christ's love?
I am convinced that nothing can ever separate us from his
love. Death can't, and life can't . . . nothing in all creation
will ever be able to separate us from the love of God that
is revealed in Christ Jesus our Lord.
ROMANS 8:35, 38-39, NLT